THE PRACTICE ROUND

*Lessons, Laughter,
and
Life's Little
Mulligans*

LEILA OWENS MORRIS

ISBN: 979-8-9927418-1-0

Second Edition

Published in the United States of America

IN LOVING MEMORY OF MY FATHER, who taught me that all of life's events—good and bad, achievements and failures—can be used as learning opportunities. He also advised that a sense of humor, especially about yourself, is absolutely essential to navigating life.

Thank you, Dad, for all the wisdom you imparted. I miss you every day.

PREFACE

This is not intended to be a literary masterpiece. This is a collection of true stories accompanied by some things that I have learned over the decades. They come with the caveat that dialogue might not be exactly accurate. Though the incidents are true (twisting the verbiage used in an iconic 1960s detective show), some of the names have been changed to protect the guilty. If anything you read sparks introspection, warms your heart, or makes you smile or chuckle, then I have achieved my purpose here. If you enjoy a good belly laugh, then this effort has been a success.

INTRODUCTION

absolutely love playing golf! It's the one competitive sport that doesn't necessarily pit you against an adversary. Your real rival is the golf course itself. The challenge to control your mind and body to achieve successful shots is, to me, both fun and invigorating.

Nothing beats walking a golf course. I love the smell of freshly mown fairways. I find it quite intoxicating. The wind always feels wonderful to me, so wonderful that I never really mind how it affects my game. I love early morning rounds when the dew is still on the greens and the beads of moisture glisten with all the colors of the rainbow as the sun begins to rise. Those colors always signal to me a promise from above, maybe a super round or a bogey-less round. Or maybe even the promise that the Lord of the universe is with me while I hack my way around the course. I love having to study the undulation of the greens and other intricate details, like how the blades of the grass are lying or how the ball sits on a tuft of grass. Awareness of the course is absolutely essential to a good score.

Not only do I love the course, I love how I feel after a round. My body has been thoroughly stretched (or contorted, whichever you prefer) from head to toes. As anyone into the game of golf knows, there is nothing that compares to the feeling of pure euphoria you get from perfectly compressing that little white ball with your six iron.

The absolute best thing about the game, in my opinion, is that before a competition or tournament—you know, when it *really* counts—you get a practice round. That means that you get to play the whole golf course and see how each hole is laid out, so you get to see where all the sand traps, deep bunkers, unexpectedly thick roughs, and water hazards are and determine what club to use to avoid them. You even get to personally witness the danger of that obtrusive tree limb hanging over the fairway which, because of its beauty, seems harmless. All of this firsthand knowledge doesn't mean that you will avoid all trouble when the game counts, but it does give you an advantage.

Life would have been easier with a practice round. To know ahead of time what traps and difficulties were ahead might have made the course of life a little easier. Alas, though, that is not the case—not how the game is played. In fact, life doesn't even come with one of those nifty scorecards that show the layouts of each hole. Life contains nothing but blind shots.

As I approach another significant birthday, I sigh with many regrets—especially my failure to follow through. Unfulfilled desires, unachieved personal goals, failed dreams, and ruined relationships all haunt me. Ruminating on all the wasted opportunities and squandered time has left me very sad in many respects. I grieve poor decisions as well as indecision.

Though I am tempted to consider my all my blunders, gaffes, mistakes, failures—whatever I choose to call them—in a bad light, instead I am electing to view this first part of my life as a practice round.

What matters at this point is how I play the remaining holes, so to speak, and how I finish.

CHAPTER 1

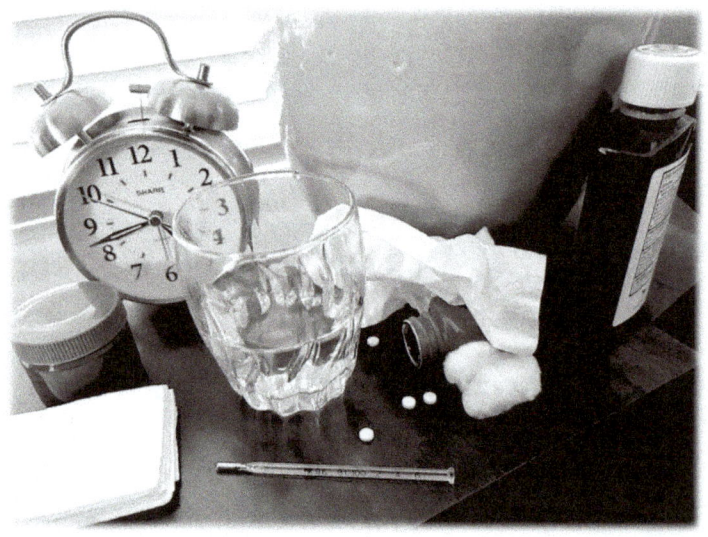

The first six months of married life flew by quickly. I was busy organizing cutlery, china, and crystal—general nesting activities. You know, the really important stuff.

Upon marriage, I moved into my husband's house—a 1970s ranch complete with 1970s decor and, as a bonus, an accompanying thick layer of dust on everything. Before the wedding, premarital negotiations allowed for removal of the lime-green velour sofa, so at least that was one particular I did not have to contend with.

The demands of work, stepchildren, and new household responsibilities mixed with the overall change in daily routines and habits were taking their toll physically. November came quickly, as well as the flu. I was seldom sick, but this came out of nowhere, hitting me fast and hard. Fever, chills, aches, and a cough got the best of me, and I left work to go home and find rest.

Since I was seldom sick, I lacked a medicinal inventory. Although my husband, Howard, was not sickly either, I looked in his medicine cabinet anyway to see what I could find that might ease my symptoms and suffering. There was no cough suppressant or decongestant to be had. In the cabinet were three pain reliever containers, all empty except for the cotton balls that were always, inexplicably, left in. I hurled those into the trash can all the while muttering obscenities. (Apparently, uttering obscenities was a condition common with the strain of flu I had.) I continued searching. Thankfully, a yellowed and crusted jar of mentholated rub was stuck to the shelf of the bathroom vanity cabinet. *That's a start*, I thought as I pried it loose.

Medicated with rub and a pain reliever recommended for menstrual cramps, I slowly moved around the bedroom in search of fleece pajamas, which, by the way, aren't readily found during the honeymoon phase of the marriage. I located and donned a sweatshirt and sweatpants then crawled into bed in search of relief.

Shortly after five o'clock, Howard made it home. He was shocked that I was in bed at such an early hour and was deeply concerned because, like I said, not only was illness rare, my being totally incapacitated was unheard of.

He gingerly placed his hand upon my forehead, simultaneously asking, "Are you running a fever?"

I responded, "Yes, it was 102 earlier this afternoon."

Puzzled, he asked how I knew for sure.

I know there are those who when feeling bad, like to be pampered. I am not one of those people. I want to be left alone, and I do not want to converse with anyone about anything. So, by this time I was getting a little impatient with his game of questions, smarted back that I had used a thermometer, and pointed to the one on the bedside table.

Howard glanced over to where I was pointing and responded, "Oh, I did not know we had a thermometer. Did you get one today when you left work?"

Another. Stupid. Question. Jeez, Louise! The tone of my response was not nice. "No, I did not. I used the one you had in the bottom of the bathroom cabinet."

Silence. At last, blessed silence. As I lay there in the quietness, however, I began to become increasingly uneasy about the old mercury thermometer I had used. Why was Howard unaware he had one? Something was instinctively troubling me, yet I couldn't quite pinpoint what it was.

After a long silence came Howard's response, and then I knew what *it* was.

"I hope you cleaned it well," he said with a smirk. "That one was used on my bird dogs."

Lesson Learned

TAKE CARE OF THE LITTLE THINGS. Failure to do so can leave you with a bad taste in your mouth.

Aside from the aforementioned euphemism that I couldn't resist using, little things—the mundane and routine—are just as important as the big things.

CHAPTER 2

married a farm boy. My husband, Howard, grew up in the 1950s and '60s. He was raised by grandparents in rural south Alabama. These hearty souls worked hard. They cleared land by hand, planted and harvested row crops, and raised different varieties of livestock both for food and for sale at auctions. They lived simply but lived well. Howard told me that they didn't have many material possessions, but they always had plenty of food on the table. They shared with others. It's true generosity, indeed, when you don't have much but share anyway.

Howard's grandparents, as well as most individuals in the community, relied on two primary sources for guidance and direction: the Bible and the *Farmer's Almanac*.

Now, I'm a God-fearing person, and if you read me something from the Bible, I will pay attention to you. I don't discount information in the *Farmer's Almanac* either because frankly, country farm people just know stuff.

Both the Bible and the *Farmer's Almanac* speak to seasons, moons, sowing, and harvesting. For those who aren't familiar with the *Farmer's Almanac*, there is one available on the Internet. Using the online version of the *Farmer's Almanac*, you are only one click away from knowing the best time to castrate your bull or slaughter your livestock. You can learn when (or when not) to mow your lawn, prune your bushes, or put up your fencing. On a more delicate level, the *Farmer's Almanac* can advise you when to cut your hair, quit smoking, and begin a diet. Apparently, there also are good and bad times to host a party and get married.

The *Almanac* is available in book format, and Howard's relatives all had *Almanac* calendars with pertinent information printed on each day about such things like the moon's rising and waning and what parts of the body the signs were in. The calendar was their immediate reference point.

Not only does the Bible have *a lot* to say about seasons, it counsels on the dangers of doing things at the wrong time. You are advised not to act too hastily, and though I've never seen the word *procrastinate* in the Bible, I have read scripture warning about the failure to act due to fear or laziness. Guilty on both counts here. Should have read the book of Proverbs much sooner in my life.

Howard knew the *Almanac* like a Southern Baptist preacher knows the town diner's daily buffet. My plans for Howard and myself were often altered because my desire to see a movie didn't coincide with the right time to treat his cattle. Apparently, if you castrate a bull at the wrong time, his testicles will draw up inside his body or keep bleeding, or maybe it was some other horrific thing that I can't for sure recollect or have blocked out. Howard said that when their cattle were free-range and branding was necessary to keep rustlers at bay, they had to brand when the moon was just right so that their brand would keep its shape and not grow or disappear. Howard and his relatives carefully coordinated the scheduling of their medical procedures to be in line with the signs. There were rules like "you can't get your heart operated on when the signs are in the groin." (Again, I might not be accurate on the specifics here!)

I once bought some azaleas (a beautiful Southern

bush), and he neglected to help me because he told me that I was planting them at the wrong time.

"If you plant when the moon is on the rise, you will have too much dirt leftover from the hole and have to haul it away," he would say. Or was it when the moon was waning? I can't remember.

Back to the story.

The dog died. Our beloved bird dog, Easy, died.

Yes, it was August in south Alabama, and the dog died. Augusts in south Alabama require the same amount of mental and physical tenacity and resilience as February requires for Wyomingites or Mainers. Overwrought with grief, I implored Howard to help with the arrangements. Yes, graveside services are always expected here.

"Howard," I asked, "don't you think we should bury the dog now?" He was in his leather chair enjoying a hunting magazine.

Howard gazed across the room, first at me, and then at the *Farmer's Almanac* calendar hanging on the wall. *Oh my*, I thought, *he* couldn't *be thinking…* He absolutely was.

Howard rose from his chair and walked across the den, right past me, to the kitchen. He studied the calendar.

"Let's seeeee," he sang, "the moon is on the decrease." He then paused and, cocked his head to the side. I knew he was, "ciphering," the term he uses when he is studying intently on something. "Soooo... if we dig and bury him today, there won't be enough dirt to fill the hole."

Seriously? I thought Howard was a graduate of Auburn University, not an attendee of Hee-Haw Academy. It was ninety-eight degrees in the shade. If we didn't borrow the freezer at the local grocery, that dog wasn't going to hold until the moon was right. There's not enough lime in the county to mitigate the stench that would resonate from the carcass in a couple of days, I calculated.

Now some might have interpreted his looking at the calendar as a convenient excuse to avoid dealing with an unpleasant chore that required immediate attention. I knew from years of watching his family refer to the *Almanac* that he took this seriously. I know he probably understood the urgency of tending to the dog's carcass, but referring to the *Almanac* was an impulse out of habit.

Realizing there were potential perils in imposing reality on an obviously delusional individual, I quickly composed myself and responded—very calmly and rationally, I might add—"Well, let's get this done today, and I will make sure I go get some dirt to fill in the hole completely."

Problem solved. We circumvented the *Almanac* and buried the dog.

Lesson Learned

PAY ATTENTION TO TIMING. Most of my life I have acted too hastily when waiting would have been the prudent thing to do. Over the years, though, I have developed some patience. I think often that it's hard to know when to wait and when to just "bury the dog." If you are unsure about timing, you just need to do the task at hand. Do the needful thing in front of you.

CHAPTER 3

The farmhouse where Howard lived as a child and a teen was very simple in design and function. The house had only four rooms: a kitchen, two bedrooms, and a living room. There were a front porch and a back porch. The house, erected in the 1920s, was not built with heating or cooling, and there was not one shred of insulation in the whole place; thus, the house could get hotter than hot and colder than cold. The outside was wooden clapboard siding. The inside was charming and quaint with yellow pine plank floors. Darkened with the years, they provided a wonderful contrast to the whitewashed wooden walls. Homemade curtains adorned all the windows and a vintage farm sink—original to the house, of course—was the focal point of the hub of the house, the kitchen.

When Howard was a young teenager, his pa enclosed a portion of the back porch to make a bathroom. Until then, they utilized washbowls inside to bathe and a privy in the backyard to contemplate. Howard said his cousin came to the place to help harvest watermelons shortly after the installation of the bathroom and said the whole thing was "mighty confusin' seein' how for years (pronounced *fur yars*) we wuz goin' outside in the field to do our bizness, and now we have to come inside from the field." Such are the consequences of progress.

I remember the very first night we spent at the farmhouse. It was hot outside, so, of course, it was also hot inside. I was thoroughly enjoying it anyway, particularly the quietness of it all. There was no distant noise of traffic nor of neighbors shuffling about—shutting doors, talking, and whatnot. To avoid adding additional heat in the already unbearably scorching house, we grilled dinner outside. Viewing the glittery stars and their brightness without the interference of city streetlights left me awestruck. I had never seen such, as our mother wouldn't let us stay outside after dark. To top everything off, cherry on the cake, so to speak, our dogs also seemed especially excited to roam without the limitations of fencing.

After a delicious alfresco dinner, we settled in the living room for conversation, which was especially enjoyable without the competition of cable television.

The windows were open, and we were breathing fresh country air. Inside the house, the old lamps cast a warmhearted, welcoming tone on the whitewashed wooden walls. Everything was serene. After each exchange of conversation, we would return to the topic of how this current experience was the ultimate of ultimates.

Then an unexpected thing happened. The house shook, and there was a knocking on the flooring coming from under the house. Then a bark, followed by a growl and more barking. It was the dogs. They apparently had some varmint trapped under the house and was harassing the sense out of it.

"What do you think it is?" I asked Howard.

"Most likely an armadillo or a possum," he responded. "Though it could be a coon."

I responded, "Strike three! Not any of those!"

I knew he was wrong on all accounts because seeping through the cracks in the pine flooring from underneath the house came this incredibly pungent odor, and I, even being a city girl, knew that smell. It was skunk spray.

The stink permeated everything in the farmhouse and everything outside of the farmhouse. Gone was the fresh country air we had been experiencing. I opened the front door to check on our beloved pets, and both dogs looked at me with euphoric expressions on their faces. Their smiles spoke volumes, as if they just experienced such happiness like never before and may never again. They both smelled incredibly horrible. Seven or eight scrubbings later, the stench was finally gone.

I went to work the next day smelling like a skunk. As I drove off to work, I kept hoping—for my coworkers' sakes—that the odor was only stuck in my nose and not in my clothes! But the dogs were still exceedingly happy!

With no city water or sewage, we depended on a pump that worked arbitrarily. I always perceived the pump to be alive and with an evil spirit, as it seemingly knew to quit running when we were lathered up for a bath or shower. The pump never decided to break down while washing dishes or doing laundry. When it would stop running, Howard would go outside in his birthday suit wielding a crescent wrench and beat on the pump a little until it would start again. A naked, suds-upped plumber is quite a sight to see! A quick learner, I studied it was best never to bathe or shower unless my repairman husband was around. One would think this was annoying, but, somehow, we always laughed about it.

Winter at the farm was a challenge. The only source of heat was the living room fireplace. The kitchen had a potbellied wood stove, but it was non-functioning. I had seen pictures of Howard, as a child, and his Pa playing checkers in front of that fireplace. Both had chins resting on hands and elbows resting on knees. They appeared to be lost into the game. Howard is fiercely competitive, and I understand his Pa was, too. There was no television in Howard's younger years, so I suppose this was the entertainment for many evenings. Not wishing to have a fire going in the house overnight, we searched for alternative methods of staying warm through the night. We found this to work. Before bedtime, we would run a scalding-hot bath, nearly boiling our skin, and then put on layers of thermal underwear and sweats. Socks and a stocking cap were indispensable. After putting on all our bedtime apparel, we would climb into bed under a layer of three to four quilts. We were successful. Most nights we stayed warm until four to five in the morning when we would awaken to an ice-cold bedroom.

One morning in particular, Howard woke me and asked, "Why didn't you close the blinds last night?" My eyes still closed, I verified that I had. He then told me the sun was blaring right in his eyes. I looked over at him, and he was right. Only the problem was not the blinds. The sun, rising in the east, was perfectly aligned with holes in both the outside and inside walls of the house and was casting a bright ray of light on his face.

We laughed and laughed at the absurdity of it all. As we laughed, our warm breath made smoke signals inside the frigid bedroom. The sight of which only brought more giggles.

Lesson Learned

THERE IS IMMENSE JOY and pleasure in simplicity.

CHAPTER 4

Most pet lovers I know have or had that one dog or cat that was particularly special. It is the one where there is this inexpressible connection, an unexplainable meeting of the minds, a soul mate of the four-legged kind. Mine was Wilson.

Wilson was the result of one brief unchaste moment between our beautiful German shorthaired pointer, and the lab-bulldog mix bitch at the farm, Lucy. Easy, our pointer was named so because as a puppy, he would leave his dog bed and climb into the easy chair. I cannot comment on Lucy's name other than "Loosey" would have been more appropriate name, as in the fifteen years I knew the dog, she was either pregnant or nursing a litter of puppies. Her sagging teats were a testament to her persistence at motherhood. Lucy's one redeeming quality was that she had an excellent nose and could blood trail a deer. Wilson inherited that trait.

Wilson grew to be an exceptionally handsome beast. Beast he was. In his prime, he weighed 130 pounds. He was powerful, had a massive chest, and was really very quick for such a large dog. His head was oversized, and his tail was long with an O-ring at the end. We would joke that he looked like Scooby-Doo with a monkey tail.

Despite his comic features, most everyone that saw Wilson bragged about his beauty and asked what breed he was, as if they imagined he was AKC registered. I remember once a couple of ladies walking in front of our house were met by Wilson who was getting to know them like dogs generally get to know people.

One of the ladies commented, "Oh, he is sooooo beautiful. What is he?"

Howard, in a serious tone, responded, "He's a ring-tailed crotch Schnüffler."

The other lady mused, "Wow, I've never seen one of those."

Howard didn't really want another dog. The only reason I got to keep him was that we were down at the farm one day, and Howard asked if I wanted to go see Easy's puppies. I consented, "Sure."

We drove to the barn area where all of the puppies

were playing and pulling on Lucy's teats. We parked about fifty yards away and climbed out of the truck. We immediately noticed one puppy, and he instantly noticed us as well. He stopped playing with the others, stared at us, then broke and ran straight toward us. I bent over to pet the puppy, and he literally jumped in my arms.

Howard said, "I guess that one's yours!"

I struggled with naming the dog. Neighbors would make suggestions, but none seemed quite fitting. After two weeks of being a nameless pup, I finally told the dog, "You're going to have to help me think of a name for you." A typical playful puppy, he usually could be found with a tennis ball. He looked at me when I spoke to him as if he knew what I was saying. The next time he looked at me with a tennis ball in his mouth, I noticed the brand name "Wilson" written across the front. *Perfect!* I thought.

Wilson turned out to be extremely smart, and he was a pleaser. If Wilson could figure out what you wanted him to do, he would do it—unlike our current dog that is belligerent and looks to please only himself.

We had trained Easy, the German shorthaired pointer, to go out every morning and bring in the newspaper. Wilson observed Easy's behavior and coveted the accolades and stroking Easy would receive every morning upon delivering the morning news to the doorstep. Wilson, younger and faster, began running out the door before Easy and took over his morning duty, putting Easy into retirement. Months later when we installed a newspaper holder at the mailbox, Wilson adapted and would pull the paper out of the holder.

Many of our friends told us the same thing—that Wilson had "people eyes." He would indeed listen and react to conversations as if he understood everything. His people eyes spoke volumes at times.

There are dozens of Wilson stories, but for the sake of brevity, I will tell just this one. Though Wilson turned out to be an exceptional hunting dog—he could blood trail deer, retrieve doves, and find turkeys in thick brush—he was basically harmless. We live on a lake, and Wilson was always kind and tender with the ducks and geese that resided on the lake. Except for one rather ornery goose that Wilson disliked (probably because of a bad attitude) and one day picked up in his mouth, transported, and relocated three houses down, Wilson had never harmed a living creature. We had Muscovy ducks nest annually in a sago palm in our yard. Wilson checked daily on the mother, the eggs, and, eventually, the hatched chicks by sticking his nose in the nest. He never alarmed the ducks, though sometimes he would chase the ducks just to make them fly. That was for sport, though, and they didn't seem bothered by it. They knew it was only a game.

Putting the farm chickens to flight also brought special delight to my dog. However, the farm rooster did not enjoy the game. The rooster, overly proud, in my opinion, would switch into an aggressive mode and challenge Wilson. When Wilson backed off, he would give a large cock-a-doodle-doo, strut tauntingly, and perch himself on the front porch bannister with his chest out. It was a gloating posture for sure.

When Howard and I would drive up to where the rooster was and let Wilson out of the truck, the rooster usually gave a crow that seemed to say, *I'm the king here!*

Evidently, Wilson disagreed. Or maybe the rooster just annoyed him.

One day, we went into the farmhouse to fix some lunch and left Wilson outside to roam the ranch. There was no sound of a disturbance, but when we went back outside, we saw Wilson on the ground with his front paws out in front of him. He was holding down a bald rooster and looked at us with those people eyes. He had rooster feathers stuck to his lips and the second biggest smile I've ever seen (second only to the expression after the skunk raid). He had plucked that bird naked except for his head and tail feathers.

The bird eventually recovered and grew back his plumage; however, from that day on, he never had that loud cock-a-doodle-doo. All that fowl could ever muster again was an *errrk*.

Lesson Learned

EVEN NICE PEOPLE DON'T LIKE ARROGANCE. (Kudos to me for not using the word *cockiness*.)

CHAPTER 5

"**D**ate fraud."

I looked at her, stunned.

"He perpetrated a fraud from the day we met until the day we said, 'I do,' and he put a ring on my finger," proclaimed my younger sister. "He was not what he purported to be."

Still puzzled, I asked, "How did he perpetuate the fraud?"

"*Perpetrate*," she corrected abruptly. "*Perpetuating* the fraud is when you stay married to the idiot."

I dared not say anything else. First of all, she is the one with the law degree, and for all I knew, there was actually a statute regarding date fraud that I wasn't aware of. Second, she's a fiery redhead with a quick mind and a sharp tongue.

This caused me to think. Is anyone not guilty of date fraud? I think we all innately want to hide our weaker selves and project an image that we think others would more readily accept.

I recall my offense in my late twenties. I was aided and abetted by a Catholic priest.

Friday afternoon, five-ish. I was visiting the

Catholic priest in the rectory next door to my parents' house. They were on a European vacation, so I went next door to have a conversation with someone other than my parents' two dogs that I was taking care of.

"What are you doing this evening?" the father asked.

"I have a date tonight." I looked over to see what the father was stirring on his stove. He was an excellent cook and was perfecting a tomato sauce to go over some pasta, and I watched him cut vegetables for his salad.

"Where are you two going?" he asked.

"He's coming here. I'm cooking supper."

The father's eyes were huge. "You don't cook."

He was right, I could cook some things but I had not yet developed a huge catalogue of scrumptious menus and I certainly didn't have anything in my repertoire that could impress Howard.

He paused for a long time looking at me. I guess he could tell I really didn't have a plan yet.

"Soooo…," he asked, "what are you having?"

Reality was hitting. Time was running out, and I didn't have a menu planned, not to mention groceries bought. I was not in panic mode yet because usually things just work out, but the gravity of the situation was becoming real.

The father said, "I tell you what. Take this twenty, and go to the store, and get me a twelve pack. It's a Friday afternoon, and most of my parishioners will be on that aisle, and I'm not in a real sociable mood this evening. If I go, I will have to chat with them. I will take care of your supper for your date tonight."

I left with his money and drove to the store. I returned to a miracle rivaling those of manna from heaven, the widow's flour and oil provision, loaves and fishes, and wine from water ones.

The father had two filet mignons in a pan on the counter. There were two whole artichokes, and he was stirring a cream sauce with his left hand and writing down cooking instructions with his right. Who, other than a servant of God, in a small south Alabama town has fillets and fresh artichokes on hand?

"I needn't even ask about a grill, should I?" proceeded the father. "Don't worry. You can use mine. Go home, and set the table. Do you have wine?"

Both were silly questions, I thought. Negative on the former, affirmative on the latter.

Five minutes before my date, before Howard arrived, the father rolled his Weber grill over and delivered the food. It turned out to be a wonderful evening, and Howard was quite impressed with my supposed culinary skills.

Of course, confession had to follow. Both for myself and the priest's and my conspiracy to perpetrate a fraud.

Lesson Learned

GOD DOES PROVIDE. He knows our needs before we do and will come through just at the right time.

CHAPTER 6

I t was our first February as husband and wife. It was early morning, and I recall it must have been a weekend because there was no urgency to awaken and rush off to work. Howard rolled in my direction, placed his arm over me, and whispered, "Someone I know has a birthday coming up in a few days."

My eyes popped open. Someone indeed, but not me. I knew his first wife had a February birthday but did not know the date. Using my rather shrewd investigative techniques, I got him to unwittingly disclose what day the festivities would be. The eighteenth. Perfect. I said nothing else.

The eighteenth arrived, and he woke early and brought me coffee in bed. The ridiculous romantic had picked a restaurant for us to enjoy, a fine-dining one. Lovely. And just when I had grown weary of cooking!

The evening came, and, I must admit, I rather enjoyed getting dressed. I had splurged on a new outfit for the special occasion and I knew spending money on my new pair of cocktail pants and cashmere sweater would be an approved amendment to the household budget once he became aware of his faux pas.

It was a great celebration full of good food, wine, laughter, and yes, a birthday present. I unwrapped it and smiled. A very nice golfing sweater. Not romantic by most women's standards, but I thought it was the perfect choice. And this one was actually the correct size! I leaned over to thank him with a kiss and then broke the wonderful news. "And we can do this again, in May, when it's *my* birthday."

Lesson Learned

SOMETIMES IT'S BENEFICIAL to not correct someone's mistake.

CHAPTER 7

had a friend once tell me that country people were experts at drinking and shooting. I believe her for several reasons. She is smart, reliable, and has firsthand experience, as she grew up in rural Alabama. I also believe her because, after my own two-year stint living in the country, I determined there is not much else to do but practice those two things.

Howard and I decided that while building our dream home, we would save money by not renting a place to live. Consequently, we loaned our furniture to my siblings to use in their houses and lived with my parents. On occasion, when relief was needed (either relief to us or my parents), we would go to Howard's old home—the farm—for respite.

August is quite unbearable in lower or coastal Alabama. The heat is draining, and the humidity is stifling. Each breath is laborious. Usually, our Augusts are somewhat rainy. The precipitation is usually accompanied by violent thunderstorms. If the rain is caused by a cool front passing from the west, relief is experienced. Thunderstorms coming from the Gulf of Mexico, however, bring only more heat and humidity, more arduous breathing, and more suffering.

It was on such an unbearably hot day that Howard and I sought relief under the shade of the pecan trees surrounding the farmhouse. The old farmhouse was not air-conditioned. In addition, the west side of the house was not protected by a porch nor shade trees, so the blazing afternoon sun would heat up the house to a temperature making it much too uncomfortable to be in until well after sunset. Conversely, under the pecan trees, the temperature averaged ten degrees cooler, and gentle wisps of breezes could be felt.

Pecan tree shade can't be fully enjoyed without the appropriate beverage. I know Southerners normally gravitate to sweet tea, but on this particular afternoon, an after-five thirst quencher was compulsory. A chilled glass of Chardonnay would have been the normal libation, but we were out—poor planning, I agree (lesson from chapter 1 not fully learned)—and the nearest grocery or liquor-licensed vendor was at least thirty minutes away. As rural folk often do, we adapted.

A quick scavenging of the pantry, refrigerator, and truck bed of Howard's GMC (yes, truck bed) gleaned a half bottle of orange juice (past expiry date), a lemon-lime sports drink, instant lemonade mix, and a half-quart gin. We perused the kitchen cabinets and found an evidently once-white Tupperware pitcher. The plastic pitcher was yellowed on the outside from years of being exposed to the afternoon sun through the kitchen windows. The tea stains inside the pitcher were a testament to the decades of family meals shared at the old home. Without measuring cups or spoons, we guessed what we believed to be the perfect proportion of each ingredient. Adding ice and a shriveled lemon from the fridge's hydrator for garnish, we had a heat-relieving, mood-altering *concoction extraordinaire.*

The sun not yet set, it was still too hot to go inside. Not that there was anything to do inside. A black-and- white rabbit-eared television complete with aluminum foil wrapped around the antennae for added reception, circa 1970, and a set of dominoes were the entertainment choices in the old house. Howard and I decided to poke around the barn.

The barn did not disappoint. It was chock-full of

antique farm tools and implements. We quickly found an old handwoven leather whip, a leather hole punch, and his pa's brand. Howard's eyes were wild with excitement with each item he found. With each tool came an explanation of how the tool was used, a "one time we…" story from his childhood working on the farm. I found all of it extremely interesting myself, excepting the cobwebs and rodent droppings. Most of the tools dated back to the 1920s. I found two items and held them up. One was a set of square sticks about one inch by one inch and maybe twelve inches long tied together at one end. The other item was an iron rod with a heavy wooden grip. The grip had splintered over the years and was being held secure by a piece of thin cord. The cord had darkened with age. I suspect the cord alone was sixty years old. The iron rod had a large pointed tip on the end. My quizzical look at Howard prompted an immediate explanation.

"Castration tools," he offered. "The iron was heated in the fire to cauterize. The sticks are to…" Well, I'll stop there.

Time passed. We looked through old hammers, rusty tractor parts, antique carved whip handles, plow disks, and evidence of contraband (old moonshine jars). Then, at last! The afternoon entertainment item was spotted! His old lasso.

Still sipping the concoction extraordinaire, we moved to the yard where Howard played with the stiffened rope. He tossed it a dozen or so times—first at the open ground and then at a fence post. He looked very inept—all the while bragging about his one-time prowess in lassoing and horse handling.

All humility gone, he bragged, "I could snag a heifer from my horse riding wide open." I was somewhat skeptical.

I don't quite remember how the conversation developed, but somehow (after several rounds of the concoction) we entered into a wager on his being able to lasso me running across the farmyard. In my calculation, he was rusty with the lasso and hadn't lassoed a moving target in over thirty years. I was exceptionally quick and agile. Bet taken!

I remember it well because the whole miserable

instance seemingly happened in slow motion. I took off running. My thighs felt sluggish, and I knew I was not near as fast as I had once remembered. Age? Additional weight? Or was this from the dismal effects of the concoction? Could the concoction have caused me to overestimate my swiftness?

I raced forward. Out of the corner of my left eye, I watched as it approached. The lasso, fully uncoiled and spread, came over my head. Almost as soon as I saw it, I stopped. Or, more correctly, was stopped. The rope hit the front of my neck, and immense pain shot through my neck and back. I guess my intuition or reflex caused me to fall to the ground. I was hurt, both physically and emotionally. Howard was oblivious that I was writhing with unbearable pain. He was in fantasy land reliving his favorite childhood moments. Howard's muscle memory from his youth took over as well. He ran to me and took the straight end of the rope to, as they say, hog-tie me. His eyes glazed over as if in a trance, he completed the job. Three loops around my ankles, and he was done. To complete my humiliation and his trip back into time,

Howard took his cap from his head and spanked me on my rear end with it.

Lesson Learned

LEARN WHILE YOU ARE YOUNG, for this is the time when learning is easiest. If you enjoy music, learn to play an instrument. Master a foreign language. Study art.

Remember, the skills and crafts you master at a young age tend to remain with you.

CHAPTER 8

Howard came in one evening and announced that we had been invited to a barn party at Dick's. Dick was a very nice man, a hardworking local farmer who had been successful in pecans, cotton, and soybeans. He was among the social elite of the community. I knew that this event was not one to miss!

Hmmmm, I thought, *party at Dick's barn.* So I asked the essential questions "What's the dress? What do I wear?"

Howard grunted. "I don't know. It's in a barn. What would you wear to my barn?"

"Well," I retorted, "your barn hasn't been adequately cleaned in a decade and is covered in rodent feces, chemicals, and fermented seed. Hazmat suit comes to mind." I ignored the glare directed at me.

I knew the dress could be anything from dungarees to sundresses, so being a cautious individual, I opted for something in the middle—a nice denim jumpsuit (quite modish at the time, I assure you) and some sandals.

The day of the grand event came. We arrived

fashionably on time, and I looked to see what the other women guests were wearing. There was quite an array of outfits, but most of the ladies were adorned in the typical Southern spring attire: fine linen, big hats, big earrings, and chunky jewelry. I noted their nails were polished to perfection. I looked down at my own feet. My toenails were embedded with dirt from my garden. Oh well. I then mastered the art of mingling while hiding my feet under tables, potted ferns, and the like.

A month later came another barn party invite. This time at Ronnie's. I would make sure I got this one right!

I am Southern, so, of course, I had a linen outfit, and now I was sure that it would be appropriate for a barn party. I upgraded my sandals to a dressier style and proceeded with the process to dig the grime out of underneath my toenails.

Now I was age forty and had never had a pedicure. There had been no need. Since I was an avid golfer and tennis player, I always had white feet. Women with white feet don't wear sandals. No need to waste money on a pedicure. This time it was different, though. I had done more yard work and been in the yard both barefoot and in sandals, so my feet were the approximate shade as my legs. I looked in my makeup kit and found a bottle of nail polish that I received as a complimentary gift for buying the other cosmetics that I actually used. Thankfully, it was a shade that would be suitable, so I began painting my nails.

I don't think I have ever done anything so hard in my life. Keeping that red paint on just my nails was far more difficult than what I saw in the commercials on television. I persisted, though, until the task was complete. When I looked at my paint job, it was similar to a murder scene.

Howard saw it and in a horrified tone asked, "What have you done to your feet? You're bleeding like a stuck hog!"

It was as if a wild animal had attacked my feet. Red, the shade of blood, was everywhere. Failure again. No sandals for this party. Espadrilles go fine with linen.

Lesson Learned

EVERYTHING DOESN'T HAVE TO BE DIY. Pay the professionals. Spring for a pedicure.

CHAPTER 9

During supper one night, my father said, "He's an enigma." He continued chewing his food, shaking his head from left to right, and his expression indicated deep thought. I studied him then began. "What's an..." But I stopped because I got his customary nonverbal response, which was a glance toward the bookcase that contained the family dictionary. "Look it up" was the standard reply to my queries for him about word meanings or other general knowledge. "You'll remember it if you look it up yourself," he would explain. Occasionally we would actually get a freebie— that is, he would tell us the meaning of a word—but that was only to provide immediate understanding to expedite the completion of his story.

I wish to interject a personal opinion here. I predict our society will likely wake up in a decade to realize that with all our technological advances, we may have crippled our children's learning. I have fond memories of using the encyclopedia to write papers. It took a lot longer to find information using that method primarily because as I was thumbing through all the massive amounts of material, I invariably found something else that I was interested in and would interrupt my research to acquire knowledge about and ponder on other topics. Same while using a dictionary. There are many interesting words to be found while looking up the one that first prompted you to look.

My father was an enigma. He was brilliant academically. A student of the law, he could remember most of what he read, learned, and where he read it. He could recall code citations. I would work for him at his law practice when his secretary was on vacation, and he would ask me to pull a book from his law library. How he knew what was in all those books still amazes me.

He was fun-loving, yet there was always a sadness about him and a stubborn refusal to recklessly abandon himself to joy or a carefree attitude. He could be silly and break into a dance if he heard music that he liked. I have a photograph of him pushing a lawn mower and dancing at the same time. Sometimes, he would see a piece of wardrobe or some item that he realized resembled a prop from a Shakespearean play and proceed to perform his own theatric production, reciting a soliloquy that he had memorized. Then, he would resume his normal persona—solemn and circumspect. An enigma.

My father radiated deep love for his family and close friends, yet he was not one for many hugs or embraces. He seemed stern and sometimes unsympathetic yet could be seen weeping when watching a musical performance. An enigma.

My father loved what he called characters. He particularly marveled at the wisdom of one of our hometown's "simple people"—the town's sidewalk sweeper. Many afternoons you could find my father on the sidewalk in front of his law office sharing a bag of roasted peanuts, conversation, and an RC Cola with him. Dad said he was full of pearls of wisdom.

I recall this in particular about the sidewalk sweeper. Local and county elections were important to the community's citizens. There were always speculations among the most educated and those considered to be the brightest as to who the winning candidates would be. The street sweeper was always 100 percent accurate on his predictions. This bewildered my father, so one afternoon during one of their "conferences" (Dad liked to keep things businesslike), he asked his friend how he always knew who the winners would be. His response was "I sweep the sidewalks." (Well, yeah.) "I notice which candidates' cards are thrown in the garbage and on the streets. Makes sense that the ones that are just tossed away aren't gonna win." This straightforward deduction would confound today's pollsters. Another enigma.

Then one day I finally understood, or at least began to understand, him. My sister and I, while cleaning out his mother's house, found a huge piece to the puzzle. Our grandmother, a sentimental pack rat, had kept since the 1940s all of our father's letters to them from World War II. The letters began when he first enlisted and continued until he finally returned home to the United States about a year after the war had ended.

We had known that our father had been a decorated soldier during World War II. We were aware that he was wounded several times, one severely enough that it was assumed he would not survive. I had heard more than once the story that a chaplain had been sent to his side on the battlefield to administer last rites, and my father told him, "Hell, I don't need you. Get me a (expletive) medic!" We had witnessed the lifetime physical limitations that his wounds had inflicted, yet until we read the letters he had written, we just didn't quite absorb his emotional trauma. The narrative we could piece together from the letters taught us much about who he really was. As we read through each letter, we could see him evolve as the war went on.

Without going into details here, let it suffice to say that his war experience, among other things, left him humble and with a deep sense of responsibility and obligation.

Lesson Learned

LOOK DEEPER INTO THOSE AROUND YOU. There's always more about them that you do not and may never know.

CHAPTER 10

I f you are really lucky, you will have an aging parent. I am very fortunate that my ninety-two-year-old mother is still with us. She says that people at her retirement complex comment often that "getting old isn't for sissies." Well, neither is having an elderly parent. They also joke that "none of us are getting out of here alive." Sadly true, but not at all sad that most still have a sense of humor.

As parents age, the conversations change. Communication becomes more difficult and louder. Most things have to be repeated, since they are either not heard or not remembered. In addition, the dialogue takes different courses. I illustrate with the following example of our telephone conversation.

Me: Hey, Mom. How are you?

Mom: Fine.

Me: Do you need anything from the store?

Mom: Depends.

Me: Depends on what?

Mom: Just depends.

Me (slightly irritated): Just depends on what?

Mom (irritated as well): Depends. I just need

some Depends [an undergarment brand].

Laughter ensued from both ends of the telephone.

I want to share a few things about my mother.

She was an excellent seamstress and made not only clothes for my sisters and myself but my father's suits, which my father insisted were so finely tailored that you could wear them inside out, and no one would know. I am privileged that she not only taught me how to sew but that shoddy work was not acceptable. Many times, she would inspect a seam of mine and hand me a pair of scissors and a seam ripper. "The material is puckered here. Do it over." It was painstaking and irritating, but she was right, and I was the better from it.

She was an excellent teacher; she was committed to her craft and devoted to her students. Trained as a journalist, she was recruited to teach in the late 1960s at the onset of integration, for the political powers at be were cognizant of the need for people without bias. Just the other week, a former student of hers commented that Mom "never saw color, only potential." I consider this the highest form of praise. For years I watched her go to school, teach, come home, and attend to family, then spend from after supper to bedtime grading her middle schoolers' English class papers. She graded and corrected everything. When we traveled on weekends to visit her and my father's parents in a town four hours away, none of us in the back seat of the Oldsmobile Delta 88 dared to complain nor argue, or we would get a stack of papers and accompanying grading key to help. Consequently, my whole family writes sentences like "They're over there with their things" confidently and error-free.

Just the other day—Mother's Day, in fact—I telephoned her. Feeling guilty that I had not called first thing in the morning, I cajoled her by saying, "I saw something this morning that reminded me of you, so I called."

Bait taken. "What?"

I continue. "I saw a mother opossum cross the street with four baby opossums on her back." Mother howled with laughter. Puzzled by her response, I thought that maybe she perceived my siblings and me like that. She was a great mother, but, clearly, teaching was her calling to which she enthusiastically directed most of her time and energy.

My mother provided meal after delicious meal for the six of us on a slim budget. Though my father did a significant amount of the cooking during the week, it was Mom's planning that kept everything rolling smoothly. I watched her frugal methods and learned. A child of the depression, she did not waste nor throw away a morsel. Mom was into recycling food long before recycling became a fad. We called her the Queen of Leftovers, for she could find a creative way to prepare any uneaten food.

My mother was, and still is, a stylish dresser and could piece together dozens of outfits with only a couple of staples. I remember to this day how my father adored her sense of style on a budget, and anytime I mentioned shopping for a special occasion, he would order me, "Take your mother."

Mother has a keen sense of humor. Our family has always joked with one another, but Mother—God love her—has been the brunt of most jokes. One morning, Mother accidentally brushed her teeth with the topical heat rub Bengay. Even a decade later my father would jokingly call her "hot lips."

One time, I made fun of her unintentionally. She was dressing to attend a bridal shower and when ready, came and stood by my sister and me who were playing on the floor. Poised in ballet's third position but with her right knee slightly bent, she asked, "How do I look?" She was wearing a turquoise chenille suit and coordinating shoes.

I examined her and responded, "Wonderful, except your hose are sagging at the knees." When she informed me that she was not wearing any hose, all I could do was roll on the floor laughing. My younger sister, who (with justified nicknames like Fang and Motor Mouth) normally had to be gagged and restrained in such occurrences, was smart enough to remain silent. I'll have you know that when I turned forty, karma kicked in. I looked at my wrinkled knees and immediately acknowledged my wicked behavior that day in the early 1970s, repented, and pleaded forgiveness.

Back to aging parents. Behaviors change. I took

Mother to a church service at her favorite place of worship. It is a grand sanctuary with gorgeous stained glass windows. Though she enjoys the beauty and tranquility of the worship place, she particularly enjoys the music of the pipe organ. And she can hear it!

We entered the church through a side door, and she found her favorite seat in one of the side wings that are perpendicular to the main center aisle and pews. She knelt and prayed. At ninety-two, she's fine with the kneeling. In my fifties, I struggle, dreading the pain I might incur if I live to be her age. Following prayer, she pinpointed her friend who was quite informed about all matters and all people. Mother reached into her purse and located her hearing aids so that she could be sure to get the incorrect gossip correct. I watched amused as dear old Mom, apparently unconcerned that I just lost my voice on the drive to church screaming conversation, thought it imperative to use hearing aids in tête-à-tête with her friend.

The liturgy began. Prayers for the people, hymns, and offertory followed. Finally, time for the sermon, and I watched Mother take her hearing aids out of her ears. My guess is she either thought she had heard it all or didn't want to be lectured to at her age. Maybe she decided that repentance at this stage of the game was a useless sacrifice. Oh well, I guess there are certain privileges that come with age.

At ninety-two, all filters are off, and Mother has acquired my father's inability to whisper in public. (Not that I think at this juncture she really tries or cares to hide what she thinks and feels). For example, while waiting for the symphony to start, a healthy-sized young girl entered the concert hall wearing a dress that was very short. Mother became the fashion police and announced that "she has absolutely *no* business wearing that outfit." During the performance, she shook her head in disapproval to the modern piece the conductor had chosen the symphony to perform. All I could do was chuckle at the thought that I would be admonished severely should I do the same.

Another conversation goes like this. Mom leaned across the table at lunch and in a very concerned voice asked my sisters and me, "Did you hear what happened to Doris?" Time seemed suspended as we waited in great anticipation for some horrific news. In an astonished tone, she continued, "Her children took away her car keys!" I did not even try to hide my sarcasm as I answered, "How dare they! She was legally blind and couldn't hear squat. Let's not even mention the mobility issues." There was laughter at the table but none of it coming from our mother. It was obvious that this was something she never thought would or could happen to her.

Well, of course it did. We decided that Mother no longer needed to be behind the wheel of a car. This decision was not made so much because of her limitations or inadequacies but more because of our current society's nonsensical need to speed in oversized vehicles while operating, illegally, an electronic communication device (texting and driving). And Mom has been punishing us ever since. The independent living facility where she resides provides a shuttle to the grocery and other shopping places. Mom absolutely refuses to ride it; instead, she insists we come and take her shopping. Wine, at the home, is called "provision" by the residents, and so she will telephone

one of us siblings and say, "I'm out of provision." That means that one of us has to leave work and drive twenty to thirty minutes to pick her up and drive her to the grocery. Really, doing this for her is not a chore; it's truly a privilege. Until.

Mother seems to always coordinate her need for "provision" with the other residents' shuttle trips. On multiple occasions, I have pulled into the grocery parking lot just ahead or behind of the shuttle. We have walked into the store as her friends were getting off the bus with their bags and baskets in hand. Mother, the polite woman she is, smiles, waves, and gives a lively "yoo-hoo" to them all. I seethe but realize it's all part of her punishment for taking away her freedom. And I love her for it. I love her for the reminder that most all her life she has been this magnificent, independent, spirited, hardworking being, and we have a part of her in us. That is both wonderful and comforting.

Lesson Learned

HONOR YOUR MOTHER. Always. Even at ninety-two.

CHAPTER 11

Howard and I had not been married too many years when he came home from work and asked me what I thought about us hosting a retirement party at our house. His secretary was retiring, and his organization's board members, as well as his fellow employees, thought the occasion warranted an intimate home setting rather than a rental hall or public dining room of some sort. I, of course, was delighted because the two to three times a year we entertained meant that the yard and house got cleaned. I also love to experiment with new recipes, and unwitting party guests are the perfect research participants.

As the great day of the party arrived, we had not yet gotten house nor yard in order. We shot right out of bed the Saturday morning of the party and manicured the yard, trimmed the overgrown bushes, then proceeded to the inside to remove the dust and pet hair that is the norm in our residence. The party food was all prepared because I enjoy that part. The cleaning? Well, no.

I guess I was preoccupied with deciding where to

hide all our clutter for the duration of the celebration because I did not see Howard don his cap and exit out the back door. I heard his truck door slam and the engine crank and ran to see if what I was hearing was really happening.

I recall gazing out the front window clutching the vacuum hose in my right hand and watching the taillights of his bass boat trailer get smaller and smaller as he ventured out of sight. I seethed. *Livid* is too mild of a word to express the dark cloud of anger which grew and grew with each passing stroke of the vacuum brush over the furniture.

To provide myself some type of immediate comfort, I quickly perused my collection of Broadway and movie musicals CDs. I saw a *Porgy and Bess* CD, grabbed it, and shoved it into the player. I then resumed the task at hand—to make our den presentable to a group of people that, frankly, I was beginning to dislike just for the sake of it. I was vacuuming like a maniac, and the anger changed to resentment of Howard's ability to schedule such an event and vanish. I then raged at my own stupidity at agreeing to host it. The antipathy grew. The music played. I sang. No relief from the anger raging within me.

Track after track played, and I continued cleaning. There was some consolation in the fact that the furniture was looking good again. I hummed as I worked. Then, much to my surprise, I began singing along with one of my favorite Gershwin songs. Problem was the lyrics coming out of my mouth were not the ones originally written.

(The following was sung to the great Gershwin tune "Can't Help Lovin' Dat Man" from *Porgy and Bess*.)

Fish gotta swim, birds gotta fly.
Sometimes I wish my husband would die.
Can't help hating dat man of mine.
I know he's lazy, not to mention he's slow.
I must be crazy not to walk out the do'.
Can't help hating dat man of mine.
When he goes awaaayeee, that's a happy daaayeee.
Then when he comes home, I'll drink some wine,
    then I'll be fine.

By this point, I had exchanged hands with the vacuum hose, and the corner attachment had become my microphone. The hose, wrapped around my neck, was my imagined feather boa. Not a dancer, I somehow developed some talent to shift my hips from side to side in an exaggerated fashion somewhat resembling an elephant's swinging trunk. I guess the tortuous yoga hip flexor exercises were really working. In my biggest, loudest Broadway voice, I brought it home, as they say.

He can come home as late as can beeee,
Or not come at all, it's okay by meeee.
Can't [breathe for drama here] help
    [another breath] hating dat man of mine.

After a couple of hours, unlike my soul, the house was spotless. Except for some dust remaining on the den lampshade, I had cleaned everything. I paused to make a decision here. Should I or should I not clean the entire lamp shade? I had used the vacuum attachment to etch a few obscene words into the dust on the oversized shade. The vulgar slurs were only visible if the light was turned on. I poured a drink, sipped, deliberated, and finally decided to do the right thing. I had a second drink.

Lesson Learned

LISTEN WELL, both to what is said and what is unsaid. Scripture teaches that we are to be "quick to listen, slow to speak, and slow to become angry." Great advice to live by. In my anger, I failed to realize what my husband, by going on a fishing excursion, was really communicating. His departure was actually an indication of his approval; we had good food, and the house was presentable. Everything needed for the party, in his estimation, was ready. My hotheadedness caused me to jump to conclusions. The result was, I made myself miserable.

CHAPTER 12

Many years ago, I was a year and a half past a cancer diagnosis, had gone through months of treatment, and was traveling with my husband to Baltimore to undergo tests that would confirm I was cancer-free.

We arrived in the city, and I, though a little nervous, was excited to be visiting for something other than chemotherapy treatments. As we waited in the hotel room for the dinner hour to arrive, I perused the visitors' guides that were available and gazed at one advertising snow skiing at a site west of Baltimore. "Wouldn't it be great if the weather were colder so we could snow ski while up here?" I asked. Howard looked at the pamphlet and commented that they did make snow, and we could try it. I thought he was just trying to appease me, as we had both listened to the weather forecast, and the high for the following day was expected to be close to fifty degrees.

Howard said, "Look, your test is at 7:00 A.M. We will be through no later than midmorning. After we get your good test results, we will just go, regardless of what the weather is going to be. Just plan on it."

Though I'm not convinced he really expected good test results, I was grateful at the optimistic language, and I knew that I wanted to get away and see some sights and that disagreeing with him, most of the time, proved to be an enormous waste of time, so I agreed.

The following morning—about ten-ish—we were driving westward with light hearts and cheerful attitudes. We sang to the radio, and I was grateful that I was released with no further treatments necessary. As we continued along the highway, the temperature in the automobile we had rented began to get very cold, and, though they had predicted a sunny day, gray cloudy skies were forming around us. The weatherman came on the radio and said that there had been an unusual change in the forecast. They were experiencing a front—seemingly coming out of nowhere—and they were now expecting snow. Howard and I just stared at each other. We were thinking the same thing. Snow!

Within the next five or ten minutes, sure enough, snowflakes were falling. At first it was light, but soon it was so heavy that the windshield wipers were barely keeping up with the precipitation. The temperature was nowhere near fifty.

Thank goodness, our destination was not too far away because the buildup on the roads was getting significant. We arrived at the ski facility.

For the next three or four hours, we skied, fell, rolled downhill, laughed, threw snowballs, and enjoyed the magnificent miracle we had just witnessed. For me, it was actually miracles—plural—for I had not been expected to live when my diagnosis was first given.

It was a joyous, special day for sure, but we were to witness one more spectacular event.

Six inches of snow had accumulated. We had rented a sedan, and we noticed that all the other vehicles at the ski resort were trucks and SUVs of some sort, and all were equipped for snow travel. We had no idea how we were going to make it back to the hotel in Baltimore. Alabamians aren't seasoned snow travelers.

Just as real worry was setting in, a snowplow pulled out in front of us and started heading down the road that we needed to be on to return. We followed.

Our day was orchestrated for us and it was absolutely perfect.

Lesson Learned

SOMETIMES, WHEN WE LET GO and step out, God can really put on a show!

CHAPTER 13

You've read about my dog Wilson, so you know that we were close.

In Wilson's later years, he needed help getting in and out of the house, as he could no longer negotiate the steps. At age thirteen, arthritis and the removal of cancerous toes left him a little immobile and unstable, so I would have to help him go up and down the steps by lifting up his hip.

One morning, predawn, Wilson hinted the need to go outside to attend to bathroom business. Normally, the process was easy-peasy. I would let him out the front door, help him down the steps, and then I would go inside and pour a cup of morning Joe. By the time I had gotten my coffee and walked back from the kitchen to the door, Wilson would be at the front steps ready to be helped in.

Then one morning, it was not easy-peasy. After getting my coffee, I opened the front door and, because it was still dark, could barely see Wilson but could tell he was wobbling out to the street. There was never much traffic in our neighborhood much less at 5:30 A.M. There were a couple of people down the street that worked in mills forty miles away and would be leaving home at this early hour, and my next-door neighbor left early to go to the gym, but other than the paper deliveryman, no one would be around.

As usual, I was still in my pajamas and had just washed my hair. My hair was wrapped in a towel, and I was housecoat-less. It being early April in south Alabama, the flannel pj's had been stored, and I was in what my mother would call my "shimmy-tail." My pajamas comprised a short shorts and sleeveless tee both out of jersey knit. The sleeveless tee, oversized when I bought it, had stretched out of shape and now disclosed parts that were meant to be covered.

I stood on the dark porch, shimmy-tailed, and called for Wilson to come back. I could see that he was now in the road. I looked around and saw no one, so figured it was safe to go out to retrieve him, as he was not coming back on his own. Calling Wilson and walking toward him, I heard it. *It* was the sound of a vehicle driving fairly fast along the street that ran in front of our house. Horrified that the driver might not see Wilson or that Wilson's lack of mobility would not allow him to avert a car, I sprung forward, reached over, and grabbed Wilson by the collar. I pulled him out of the road into our driveway by the mailbox just as the vehicle was turning the curve between our house and our neighbor's.

The vehicle came our way then stopped by the mailbox because it was the paper deliveryman, and he wanted to put our newspaper in the chute attached to the mailbox. Meanwhile, I was there trying to hold the dog, keep the towel secured around my wet hair, and hide the parts of my body that were intended to be covered. For what seemed like an eternity because his jeep headlights were glaring me in the face, the deliveryman put the newspaper in a plastic bag then inserted it into the place it belonged on the mailbox post, greeted me with a "mornin'," and drove away.

Initially embarrassed, I then convinced myself that I didn't know that person nor did he know me and that I would never see him again. Wilson and I returned to the house and stepped inside.

Later that morning, at work, I was in the mailroom

checking my mailbox and overheard a very interesting conversation.

"Well, Jerry, how's the route going?"

Jerry answered, "Great, so far."

"Do you have enough time to make all your deliveries and still get to work on time?"

"Yes, it's working out great, and I'm going to enjoy the extra spending money. It wouldn't take any time at all except they want all the newspapers put in a plastic bag to protect them from the rain or dew."

I felt sick. My eyes grew big. I felt my face turning flush, and I turned to look at Jerry, who grinned and winked. "Mornin' again."

Lesson Learned

LIVE AS IF SOMEONE YOU KNOW IS ALWAYS WATCHING because someone always is.

CHAPTER 14

Women love games. That's not rhetorical. They love cards and parlay and particularly enjoy the exchange of gossip (err, I mean exchange of unverified information) during the games. My mother once told me that women can get mean when they play bridge; so, since I am basically nonconfrontational in nature I have not learned the game. I have friends who enjoy Bunco, but the game brings out the demons in me. Gin Rummy is ok, but it's not my favorite. I absolutely love the Worst Gift game. I always win.

Here's how the game is played. It begins with a bottle of wine, at least four glasses (meaning four players, not four consumed), and conversation. I've never been a great conversationalist. I'm not a chatty person. My father's side of the family has zero social skills. I inherited all of them. In addition, tête-à-tête topics among most women absolutely bore me or are completely irrelevant to my life. But statistically speaking, women's exchanges almost always ultimately drift to the topic of husbands or significant others, their merits and failures.

Round one began.

"My husband gave me socks for Christmas."

The shameful shaking of heads, sneers, and piteous looks granted the first player were horrific. I thought, *Socks would be great! Especially wool socks, the thick kind that feel good in front of a fireplace on a cold night while you are enjoying a nice glass of wine and the serenity of the house to yourself while your husband is off hunting. Is that your best?*

Player two of round one. "I got a Bundt pan once."

I was alert. Not a great gift, but certainly not merit worthy, or could it be? I studied the competition. Their poker faces couldn't hide the fact they thought this was worse than the socks.

Player three complained about the necklace of cubic zirconia that was handcrafted but looked as if it were found in the toy section of the dollar store. Heads cocked as if to say, *Well, he tried.* In my estimation, the others definitely didn't feel too sorry for number three.

My turn. I was confident. I was thinking I only had to trump the Bundt pan.

Of course, the fact that in twenty-nine years of marriage, my husband has never bought a Christmas gift earlier than on Christmas Eve gives me a great advantage in the game.

Strategy is important. I have an inventory of a score of potential winners, but knowing your competition is crucial. *Should I use the .243 rifle?* The gift was a definite loser in my book, but I had hunting friends who would think it fabulous. I carefully analyzed. Player number three was not a big hunter but lived on a ranch and ran a hunting guide service with her husband. She just might think this was cool. Not the best move. The two dozen outfits purchased in the "size that I should be?" Errant, but not bad enough to win this round. Perfume that reacts with my acidic body chemistry resulting in a putrid odor. I have a total of sixteen bottles received and never used because Howard can't remember that I can't wear perfume. Again, good intent on his part, so I probably can't ensure a victory with that choice.

I selected and played my move. Howard specially ordered this for me and was exuding joy when it was delivered.

I looked around the table and confessed, "I was once given a fat-reducing kit."

Faces disclosed the shock they were feeling and total disdain for my husband. I continued, "It was a box with a miracle gel to put on the waist, complete with its own specially designed spatula for applying the gel, and a belt to be wrapped around the abdomen to 'melt that unsightly, unwanted belly fat,' or so the advertisement and instructions on box instruction said."

Three wine glass stems hit the table at one time. "You win!" they exclaimed in unison.

Lesson Learned

YES. It most definitely can be much, much 'better to give than receive'! Other than that, I can't think of a single one.

CHAPTER 15

I usually go to the symphony alone.

I don't really *want* to go alone. Ideally, I would want to be accompanied by my husband, walk into the concert hall arm in arm or hand in hand, enjoy a cocktail during intermission and all the other things I see most other couples do. I imagine looking fabulous in that little black dress and having my husband lost in my eyes. In this case, reality doesn't meet expectation.

I should have realized this in the dating stage of our relationship. We were exploring each other's worlds. I was learning how to herd cows and put up barbed-wire fencing, and he was being exposed to golf and cultural events.

Our first cultural outing to the symphony was stressful. Accounts of the first event follow.

Since Howard's work was largely outdoors and with farmers, he mostly wore blue jeans. Work meetings occasionally warranted khakis and a long-sleeved button down, but I had never seen him wear a sport coat, much less a suit. Howard ensured me that he was excited about the concert and that he would finally get to wear his suit again. He expressed delight at the thought of pulling out the baby-blue polyester leisure suit. I cringed. I backpedaled and tried to think of how Emily Post might retract an invitation. My parents, however, had raised me to be humble, not to judge people, and never ever look down on anyone for any reason. So, I waited in dread for the moment he would pick me up for our date. I exhaled an immense sigh of relief when I opened the door and saw him attired in handsome gray slacks with an accompanying stylish navy sports jacket grinning from ear to ear that he had pulled one over on me.

I did not know, however, the excitement for this evening was just beginning. As the symphony warmed up, we enjoyed casual conversation. I learned that he had played the piano in church, mastered the accordion, and had suffered through violin lessons. But, as he explained, the violin "put a crick in [his] neck so [he] told [his] pa [he] wasn't havin' anymore of that." The symphony quit its cacophony of random scales and excerpts from the program to come. Howard slowly began rising out of his seat, simultaneously spreading his hands, signaling an approaching applause. I gasped; then, out of instant reflex, I grabbed him and pulled him to his seat. He grinned at me and said, "Gotcha!"

Another outing a year later, we went to a production of *The Music Man*. He thoroughly enjoyed that performance but complained that I should have splurged on better seats for, as he said, "somethin' that good."

I had always dreamed my husband would exhibit many, if not most, of the admirable qualities of my father. Unfortunately, the only characteristic Howard and my father seemed to have shared was the inability to whisper in a public setting. My father's whispers in church could be heard four pews up and four pews back.

Cue next performance. It was a combination of Broadway and famous operatic tunes sung by a trio of baritone, tenor, and soprano. The vocal talents as well as the orchestra were marvelous. Howard was less than enthusiastic about going, and to complicate matters, he had fished in a bass tournament that day.

To those of you unfamiliar with bass tournament fishing, it is an all-day affair requiring a waking time of three in the morning and fishing from safe daylight (in this case, 5:30 A.M.) until about three or four in the evening. Howard was beyond tired and kept dozing off. I was annoyed, of course, because musical outings were a rarity for us (unlike his fishing tournaments).

Then came intermission. Snooze over. We watched as most rose from their seats to stretch and find relief at the bar or restroom. One man about three rows up stayed motionless with his head down. *Ah*, I thought, *at least my husband is not the only one sleeping.* A slight smile came across my face at the realization that I might not be the only one escorted by a Rip Van Winkle. Minutes passed and he still did not move, and concertgoers were all whispering to locate a physician. The gentleman seated right behind us announced, "I'm a doctor," and proceeded to the man in the slumped, sunken position. In only seconds, he walked back shaking his head and whispered to his wife that the man had passed away. Howard, in his

NON-whisper, exclaimed, "He's the lucky one."

Then came the straw. You know, the camel's back breaker.

Date for the opera. Howard promised no fishing, though he was going to work for a while at the farm, and we planned a nice evening out; we would have dinner then enjoy the performance. Again, my expectations far exceeded what really happened.

I washed my hair, painted my nails (which was a big deal for me), and pulled out that little black dress that I had been waiting to wear. Four o'clock came, and Howard was nowhere to be found. This was pre–cell phone time, so I couldn't figure out what was happening. Time passed. At five thirty, he came running in the door and headed for the shower. Though I knew he was really too late for us to have a nice dinner, I did not say anything. We got in the car, and he drove. It was a thirty-minute drive to the city where the opera and nice restaurants were. "What time is the performance?" he asked. "Seven thirty," I reminded him. Silence followed. He was, again, "ciphering." Not enough time to go to the romantic restaurant in an Antebellum home that specialized in French cuisine. Not enough time to go to a fine steak house. Not enough time to dine out anywhere nice.

As we continued driving, the opportunities for decent dining as compared to fine dining were diminishing. He knew it as well and turned the vehicle into the last and only dining opportunity (of any level) available—an establishment known for extraordinarily "gifted" women wearing tight and revealing tops and short shorts. I, in my little black dress with the painted nails and rhinestone earrings, was overdressed, in every sense of the word, for this restaurant, or dive, or hellhole. I was heated much hotter than the chili that I choked on for supper.

Finally, we arrived at the theater. I, vowing that nothing was going to ruin Puccini's *Tosca*, tried to forget the previous three hours and the dismal dining experience and enjoy the rest of the evening. The opera guild of this small city had a reputation for excellent quality, and that night was no exception.

After I had adjusted my attitude, I noticed Howard. He was actually quite amusing to watch. His head was bobbing up and down between the superti-tles offered above the stage and the synopsis con-tained in the program.

The final straw. *Tosca*, act 3, the final aria. Howard (in a very audible voice) declared, "Jump! Now! Pleeeeease!"

Lesson Learned

GO TO THE SYMPHONY ALONE. It's okay.

CHAPTER 16

Another Christmas. Another doling out of assignments for the family holiday feast.

My older sister, who always manages to get her way, won the entrée nomination of rib roast, knocking out my beef Wellington. Instead, I was relegated to my customary oyster pie. A great dish, for sure, but one I could make blindfolded. I wanted a change and a challenge.

"Pleeease let me bring something other than rolls," cried my younger sister. The family was gathered and was voting an overwhelming no. Even my father, who is normally laid-back and supportive of our endeavors, was behind her shaking his head.

The catalogue of my younger sister's gastronomic catastrophes was extensive. Included among the most memorable were the Key-Lined Pie, the Fireball Cheeseball, and the Jalapeño to the Third Power Spinach Madeline.

We thought that assigning a pie to li'l' sis would mean that she would go to the freezer section of her local grocery and select one premade. No. The overachiever, competitive gal attempted her first key lime pie. Actually, it was quite tasty, but she failed to take the plastic lining off the graham cracker crust prior to adding the filling.

Then for a cocktail-hour hors d'oeuvre, she brought a cheese ball. The outside was supposed to be covered in pecans and paprika. She substituted cayenne pepper for the paprika. I guess in her mind they looked the same; both were red. Guests were sweating bullets and wishing for a wine-to-water miracle.

Finally, the colorectal nightmare. The exponentially calamitous Jalapeño to the Third Power Spinach Madeline. The recipe called for jalapeño seasoning and Monterey Jack cheese. Instead of just plain Jack cheese, she used Pepper Jack cheese. Tums was the desert of choice after this side dish was eaten.

It really wasn't her fault. Except for breakfast, which we took turns cooking, none of us were allowed in the kitchen when meals were prepared. This was my parents' time to discuss matters of importance and come to a meeting of the minds in family matters. Instead, we were given chores like setting the table and cleaning the kitchen.

When celebrating special events, my younger sister and I would make place cards. Initially we were writing the names of the family on each card. Later, we became more creative and drew caricatures of the family members. Each person would have to determine their seat by identifying the appropriate unflattering drawing with exaggerated features. We quit the year when we were trying to draw my father's mother, and the drawing kept resembling our other recently deceased grandmother. Creepy. That's entirely another story.

My mother and my father entertained regularly. They were a good team at a lot of things, and planning and executing a dinner party was one of them. My father was the better cook of the two, and he was exceptional at planning a menu. I remember as a child, I hid under a table, completely obscured by the overhanging tablecloth, during the drinks and appetizers course of one of their functions. (Children then, according to the rule, were to be seen and not heard.) My father had a collection of fifty shot glasses, each unique in shape and design, and each one was partially filled with cocktail sauce. He had fresh raw oysters on ice and was scooping oysters out of the shell and placing the oysters in the shot glasses for his guests who would quickly slurp them down and follow them with a saltine cracker. The atmosphere was entirely friendly. These were Second World War and Depression survivors. They had seen hard times and evil times. Most had witnessed, firsthand, death and destruction. To them, life was too short for pettiness. Unlike some of my contemporaries, the mothers steered from catty behavior or jealousy of others. Men were comrades still. Even as a child, I could feel the love in the atmosphere. It felt like a real party should.

I recall another event years later when I was a young teen. My father had prepared a dish called "Chicken Beulah." It was a very cheap dish to make. Chicken, pasta, and pimento were the main ingredients, but my father had engineered a delectable cream sauce to make it a culinary masterpiece. Since he prepared the meal, my mother exercised her forte as a hostess and table decorator to create the right ambiance. Since this was entertaining on a budget (my older sister was in college), she asked me to go out-side and gather clippings from an Aucuba bush. I did as I was instructed, and she placed the clippings in an extraordinarily beautifully cut glass bowl. Those were ultimately placed in the center of the table.

The party went off, as they say, without a hitch. Since I had promised to behave myself, I was allowed to stand to the side of the dining room with a pitcher of water and refill glasses as needed. I did an excep-tional job, I must say, and got nods of approval from both the head of the table (Dad) and the other end (Mom). The guests were enjoying lively conversation when I noticed the Aucuba leaves of the centerpiece moving. I was frozen, not knowing what to do. I had promised no disruptive behavior. My eyes, I'm sure, were big. There was a huge green tree frog perched on one of the leaves.

Thankfully, one of the guests asked for more wine. My father got up to serve her and looked at what I was staring at. He saw what I saw. When he returned to his seat, subsequent hand and eye signals similar to Morse code and other communication (perhaps somewhat telepathic) between my mother and my father transpired, and Mom then spotted the hideous amphibian. It was about that time that the sticky-toed creature leaped from the Aucuba leaf up onto the chandelier. My quick-thinking mother, in all her Southern graciousness, smiled and suggested to her guests that the living room would be a delightful place to enjoy desert. Disaster averted.

When we were young, my older brother and my older sister were smarter than my younger sister and me. When we had family holiday celebrations, they managed to evade the kitchen area until mealtime. That was okay because they had their contributions that were just as important as the cooking. My older sister was an exceptionally talented pianist with a beautiful soprano voice, and my brother was gifted with an amazing tenor voice. They were the leaders in the family sing-alongs. My little sister and I filled in the middle as alto and second soprano. We all blended beautifully. Harmony in life is essential, you know.

Back to my younger sister's cooking.

She has progressively gotten better. We prepared

a dish together at the farm a few Thanksgivings ago. She wanted sweet potatoes, so she brought the frozen orange discs and only a little butter to dab on the top.

"I had marshmallows on the grocery list," she assured me. "I don't know what happened."

Realizing she needed to add more to the dish, we foraged together to find something to enhance her yams. I suggested we go outside and pick up pecans from under the trees. While she worked on that, I looked in the pantry and found some cinnamon (circa 1983), and there was some brown sugar in a somewhat aged box in the refrigerator.

I continued my search through all the cabinets in the farm kitchen. No one was currently living in the house, so many of the food inventory was actually outdated and in need of discarding. If I saw something with an expired date, I tossed it into the garbage. Meanwhile, sis shelled and picked the pecans.

Then I found the perfect ingredient. "Got it!"

"Got what?"

"This!" This was an aged pint of Bourbon. We added some to the yams, butter, cinnamon, brown sugar, and pecans. The yams were scrumptious and completely consumed. The only drawback was the effect of the aged alcohol. Guests were too drunk to leave.

Thankfully, my youngest sister has mastered what has become her dish for all family functions. She makes the very best green bean casserole I have ever had. In fact, in 2018, when the inventor of the green bean casserole passed away, my eldest sister contacted us all and suggested that we should bow our heads in a moment of silence in gratitude for the profound influence she had on our lives.

Lesson Learned

FIND WHAT YOU DO WELL and contribute to the feast.

CHAPTER 17

Howard and I were getting ready for work one morning, and as I finished applying my makeup, I looked in the mirror first and then at my husband and asked, "How do I look?" Rather pleased with the fact I was having a good hair day, I waited for what I thought for certain would be accolades.

"You look the same."

I have to admit his response was befuddling. I prodded, "Same as what?"

"You always look the same. You look the same whether you spend three minutes on yourself or thirty."

For convenience's sake and to avoid a tiff, I elected to view that as a compliment and from then on have invested minimal time in primping. I ended the conversation. "Well, then three minutes it is!"

Three minutes for hair and makeup plus the additional four to select and put on apparel had worked well for most of my life. Until it didn't.

For most of my working life, I had to leave the house before 7:00 A.M., and for much of that time, I was on the road by six thirty. On the contrary, my husband's work was always a five or so minutes' drive away, so he was privileged to get to sleep later. Follicly challenged, his hair care time is two and a half seconds. The considerate soul I am, I seldom turned on the lights to get dressed. Four minutes putting on clothes in the dark can result in some wardrobe horrors.

I recall a very important conference with political figures. As I was organizing my notes, I looked down to realize I was wearing pumps of different colors, a blue one and a brown one. *Well*, I assured myself, *at least they both match my skirt.* During the obligatory salutations and handshakes, I made a concerted effort to keep eye contact so theirs would not drift downward to notice my feet.

Another disaster. I had borrowed a dress from my mother for an important work event. She, as I have written, was very vogue in dress. This piece was a fuchsia knit shift. It had a double column of coordinating buttons down the front and a square neckline. I eased it on one morning, and the fit was perfect. At the end of the day, I dropped over to her house to pay a visit and share the details of what I considered a very successful day.

She greeted me with a warm smile and asked, "How was your day? And why are you wearing my dress backwards?"

She explained the buttons were to go down the back, and what I thought was a square neckline was a design to show off the back. Since I had dressed in the dark, I failed to notice the tag, which, as my mother taught me, "always goes behind." I was disappointed beyond measure primarily because it fit better the incorrect way.

Working at different locations during the week does have its perks. You can opt to wear the same outfit multiple times during the week.

I recall a beige nubby knit dress that I absolutely loved. No doubt it was one of my favorites ever! No buttons or zippers, it slipped on with ease. It was thick enough not to warrant a slip underneath but breathable enough to allow me to tolerate the torrid summer days in the south. The pièce de résistance of the wardrobe item was that it was wash, tumble dry, and wear. I wore it with a faux alligator belt that matched faux alligator shoes. Coupled with a blazer, even I managed to look professional.

Wednesday morning one week, I reached down and picked the beige dress off the floor in the exact place it lay when I took it off the preceding day. The fabric was miraculously wrinkle-free after only two shakes. I was almost out the door when my husband pointed out that I wore the fave outfit the previous day. I shot him a grin and reminded him that I was working at a different location than the day before, and nobody there would know. I added that unless there was some mishap involving a food or drink spill, the beige dress would be my attire again tomorrow, since I will be in yet another town.

I skirted (pun intended) through this behavior through an entire summer. The procedure "pick dress up off floor, put dress on, wear dress, take off dress, leave on floor overnight, and repeat steps for two more days" went on incident-free except for one time.

As I was gobbling down breakfast one morning, Howard walked into the kitchen and glanced my way.

He offered, "You look good today, but that scratching is unladylike."

Indeed, I was scratching. I felt little twinges around my waist, then my thigh and under my breast. Each time I felt what seemed like a little bite, I would scratch. Running late and in a hurry, I didn't pause to investigate. I headed straight to work to prepare for a meeting.

I guess I thought that the itching would subside, but I was incorrect in that assumption. The meeting, beginning at nine, proceeded on schedule, and I twitched, rubbed, clawed, and scratched for an hour and half. I thought I was being discreet and perhaps no one was really paying attention, but the attendees on either side of me moved their chairs two feet away as if I had some type of communicable fungus. Those seated across the table from me looked very concerned, perhaps questioning my mental state.

After a miserable day, I drove home only to enter into a house that smelled of bug spray.

Upon seeing my upturned nose, Howard enlightened me. He had found black ants on the bedroom and the master bath floor.

"Don't leave your wet towels on the floor," he chastised. "That draws in the ants."

I took off the fave dress only to find dozens of tiny little ants. Some were entangled in the nubby weave, and others were smashed on the inside of the dress.

Lesson Learned

APPLY LESSON LEARNED in Chapter 1.

CHAPTER 18

One job that I had as a young adult involved a thirty-mile commute. Half of my drive was on a two-lane then four- lane county road. For the remaining ten to fifteen miles, I accessed the interstate that took me directly into the city.

If you've driven a regular morning commute, you've most likely experienced meeting the same individuals at the same places at approximately the same time every day. It's quite fascinating, actually. My experience was no different.

I am not a fast driver. I rarely exceed the speed limit for two reasons. One, I'm too cheap to risk paying a ticket, and second, I am superstitious that Providence disappears when I am willfully disobeying the traffic ordinances.

Such was not the case of my supervisor, Ron.

Every morning I would watch in my rearview mirror as he, driving his white sedan, came quickly approaching up the rear. He weaved from lane to lane, never opting to use his blinkers, and would blow past me driving at least fifteen to twenty miles per hour faster than I was. As he passed, he would throw his chubby little hand up in a wave.

I loved Ron as a supervisor. He never disciplined or demeaned any of us in front of others. Also, if he was correcting you about something you could easily get him off topic because he loved gossip.

You could begin, "Hey, by the way, have you heard…?" Ron would then be drawn off topic and completely forget what he was chastising you about. He would then lean in towards you and ask inquisitively, almost in a whisper, "No, I hadn't heard. Tell me more." Reprimand obviated.

Ron was fun loving. The male equivalent of an 'old maid', we were his family. He made sure there was not a holiday, wedding, or birth that was not properly acknowledged and, if warranted, celebrated. On Fridays he insisted we all eat together. He would have us all pile into a car together and ride to a place for us all to enjoy a meal together. Of course, no one wanted him to drive. Everyone would cheerfully offer their vehicles for the noon excursions.

I was not the only worker that was driving this route. There were others, and the other coworkers complained how this man would often cut right in front of them, leaving little time or space for accident prevention. Defensive driving was obviously nothing Ron was concerned about. Ironically, Ron would show up to work irritated and would spend the first thirty minutes of the day ranting about all the idiots on the road.

Many mornings when we arrived in the city, we would all be stuck together in traffic even though he had driven faster than we had. I recall one particular morning, after our supervisor won the race on the interstate, we still all walked into the office at the same time.

"Stoplights. The great equalizer," exclaimed one of my coworkers.

How profound.

And, sadly, Ron died at a relatively young age.

Death. The great equalizer.

Lesson Learned

S INCE WE ALL HAVE THE SAME ULTIMATE DESTINATION, pay close attention to the journey. Remember, there are others on the highway who are trying to reach their destination, too. Always be mindful and considerate.

CHAPTER 19

Many golfing clubs have a pub or restaurant they call the nineteenth hole. This is the place where players converse, enjoy libation, glory in the magnificent shots, and bemoan the miserable ones.

This chapter is my nineteenth hole.

I have not yet addressed any golf achievements or disappointments. My greatest on course disappointment was losing my flight in a state championship by missing a one-foot putt in match play. Lesson learned: practice the routine. Over and over.

My most memorable golfing moments have little or nothing to do with how I played, but instead have to do with who I shared a round with. I have fond memories of walking the course sharing conversations with people I loved and admired. I especially enjoyed playing with my older brother. He was very good, and he was knowledgeable about the game and making shots. He was generous with his knowledge.

I also enjoyed the day I substituted a trick ball for my older sister's real ball on the green of her home course. The ball I used would skirt erratically left and right and she kept re-reading the green and practicing her putting stroke. The laughter we shared when she finally got it in the hole and discovered it was a trick ball is unforgettable.

The greatest shot I ever witnessed. My family was playing a scramble together and my father, in his sixties, and somewhat crippled from war injuries, was on our team. He pulled an approach shot thirty yards to the left of the green. His ball bounced off the bathroom shed and onto the green a mere two feet from the hole. Again, laughter.

I began a quest about forty years ago to find love and to know and understand God. I remember after work one day, I stopped by the little nine-hole course I regularly played. It had not been a great day, personally or professionally, and as I set my stance and checked my grip, my mind drifted to the difficulties of the day. Muscle memory, of course, took over on my swing, but my heart, mind, and soul were thirsty.

The magic in life was gone. Maybe, like in a golf swing, I had just lost my rhythm, but something for sure was out of sync. I was not feeling the joy, love, and excitement for life I once had. *Why?* I wondered.

As I walked the course, I was consumed with deeper questions than my swing plane or reverse weight shift on my back swing. Where had the love gone? Where was the God I'd always worshipped? I couldn't feel either anymore. Both love and what I believed to be a gracious god seemed very remote and elusive.

And such was my prayer during the closing putt of that round that day—to know and understand more deeply our great God, to achieve perfect love, and to determine the best way to live the glorious gift of life that our creator had blessed me with.

After the prayer? Lots of struggles, disappointments, seasons of failure, and dark situations. I seemed to stay in the rough, not the fairway, in the course of life. An odyssey.

This practice round had taken me over forty years to complete.

Where is God? I spent decades struggling to find Him, learn about Him, and understand Him. Now that the struggle has subsided, I realize that He was with me as a child when I used to play in my backyard.

He was with me on rainy summer afternoons on the screened porch of my grandparents' home, playing jacks, solitaire, and pick up sticks. He was with me all the times I walked the golf course. He showed up to rescue me in times of trouble. To me, God is peace; and I discovered He is available anytime I want him. I need only 'be still' and call to Him.

And love? I have learned love. Please notice I didn't say I found love or feel love. I know from the book of Corinthians that love is patient, kind, humble, unselfish, and forgiving. Thanks to my practice round, I have learned those things—kindness, patience, and unselfishness. I'm still practicing forgiveness, especially for myself.

My father was right. Every moment can be a learning experience—the wonderful warm moments and the painful ones, the successes and the blunders, the proud and the embarrassing.

I am grateful this practice time has taught me how to finish my game and finish it well. I am walking away with the ultimate prize of the powerful and eternal force of *love*.

www.ingramcontent.com/pod-product-compliance
Lightning Source LLC
Chambersburg PA
CBHW061648120626
46550CB00003B/867